THE HEARTS SPEAK

AF569251

SANAIE MEHVISH

Copyright © Sanaie Mehvish
All Rights Reserved.

ISBN 979-888546134-4

This book has been published with all efforts taken to make the material error-free after the consent of the author. However, the author and the publisher do not assume and hereby disclaim any liability to any party for any loss, damage, or disruption caused by errors or omissions, whether such errors or omissions result from negligence, accident, or any other cause.

While every effort has been made to avoid any mistake or omission, this publication is being sold on the condition and understanding that neither the author nor the publishers or printers would be liable in any manner to any person by reason of any mistake or omission in this publication or for any action taken or omitted to be taken or advice rendered or accepted on the basis of this work. For any defect in printing or binding the publishers will be liable only to replace the defective copy by another copy of this work then available.

Contents

Foreword *v*

Acknowledgements *vii*

About The Author *ix*

1. Quotes By Sanaie Mehvish 1
2. Red 4
3. Bleeding In Kashmir 5
4. Teacher For Me 6
5. Be A New Person 8
6. Home Safety For Kids 10
7. My Self 11
8. O ! Great God 13
9. Trouble 15
10. The Annual Examination 16
11. I Ask 18
12. Keep 19
13. The Mother 20
14. The World And My Heart 22
15. Eid 23
16. Today 24
17. Mehvish's Philosophy Of Life 25
18. Come Back Home 27
19. A Midnight Call 30
20. Message For Men 31

Biography Of Mehvish Maqbool Sanaie 33

Contents

Life And Philosophy 35

Foreword

Poetry is anything that touches our hearts, moistens our eyes or blossoms our lips .I have read somewhere that prose is meant for ordinary minds, whereas poetry is meant for extraordinary minds. Understanding poetry is not everyone's cup of tea. Poetry contains magical powers .It is able to inflict deep wounds on the sensitive hearts.It is also capable of healing rotten and incurable wounds. Different types of poetry serve different purposes. I am a regular reader of the poetry of Mehvish Maqbool Sanaie and I have observed meticulously the themes and topics of her poetry. She writes mostly on philosophical,social, romantic,political,educational ,recreational and contemporary issues.She has a well command over English language.The book in your hand is the solid proof of all my claims .The beauty of words , the beauty of literary devices, the exalted imagination, the tender emotions, the gift of creativity, the wisdom, all have been combined together to create the masterpiece titled " The Heart Speaks ".

If I say that Mehvish Maqbool Sanaie is a mystic of ,21st century, I won't be lying .

Without stalling you here any further, I want you to begin reading this outstanding book and I wish you a happy reading!

Nuzhat jan
Lecturer
G.A sahara public high school

Acknowledgements

I have been reading poetry of local, national and international poets from my school days. I don't know why but it is a fact that poetry is my weakness as well as my strength.I can be persuaded to empty my whole wallet to a needy person on a road with just a couplet.At the same time , i can be motivated to beat the hell out of a bad person with just a verse.Poetry controls me like a robot is controlled with a remote control.

I am grateful to my colleagues, friends, siblings who listen to me passionately whenever i recite my poems to them, even though, most of them want to murder me at times.You know ,the people of this country, unfortunately , are not great lovers of poetry...

Next,I thank my extended family (followers on social media) who regularly encourage me to continue writing poetry with their generous LIKES and COMMENTS.

I owe a big "Thank You" to (String Production) that made my dream of publishing a book of poetry come true.

Finally, i give my heartfelt thanks to my Almighty Allah, my close friends Sahil Sharifdin Bhat, Fajr, Rubeena, owais,ubaid ,Nuzhat,and all other friends who constantly boost up my morale to keep writing things and tolerate me in my worst mood swings...

Sanaie_Mehvish

About The Author

SANAIE MEHVISH

Mehvish Maqbool Sanaie is a poetess, quote, writer, historian, blogger, Gymer. She is a growing versatile personality.While in the state of Jammu and Kashmir the youth are in a dilemma whether to support the people who want freedom for the state or to cooperate with the Indian government ruling the state since 1940's ,Mehvish is inviting the youth to shun the violence and work for the peace and progress of their families, Muslim community and the whole world.She uses her poetry as a vehicle to spread the ideas of love, justice, kindness,happiness,peace,and modernity, among the people around . She is very concerned about the increasing rate of suicide and depression patients in the valley.Her principle is 'to act locally but think globally'. She particularly wants the youth of Kashmir to study hard and build their health to the maximum limit possible. Her quotes are worth writing in diamond ink. She has written somewhere that " where there is a pain, there is a lesson

And

Where there is a lesson, there is a life".

ONE

QUOTES BY SANAIE MEHVISH

"LET GO You must let go of what holds you back from living your greatest life so that you proceed."

"Detach yourself from the things and people that weigh you down and hold you back from living a life of greatness."

"Absorb what is beneficial, discard what is not, and add what is uniquely your own."

"Empty your mind and be free, forgive, forget, move on, let go, yesterday has been and gone, there is no benefit in dwelling on the past, it is a new day, so begin again."

♡♡♡

"The memories of the past hold many back, past failures, past defeats, past pains, past struggles, past adversity, and past disappointments. It does not matter what happened yesterday, if you knew better you would have done better, so let go."

♡♡♡

"Power is nothing without control."

♡♡♡

"Responding to everything doesn't mean you are brave and ignoring some things doesn't mean you are weak."

♡♡♡

"You do not become a winner by fighting every war. Sometimes it's better to be peaceful than to be right."

♡♡♡

"Never allow anyone to bully you into permanent silence but when you're short of words use SILENCE."

ÞÞÞ

"When people ask you stupid question and you don't feel like answering, just smile at them and walk away.,Sometimes SILENCE hits harder than a SLAP..."

ÞÞÞ

"Don't die before death dear friends! Just live your Temporary life on this Temporary planet.....Because no one is going to live permanently here...So, where there are struggles ,There is actually True life.....and where there r no struggles ,there is no true life."

ÞÞÞ

"Live the "JOY" of anticipation for your amazing ambition and be sure that you will reach your destination, no matter how long the "ROAD" takes you!"

TWO

RED

Red color heartbreak,
Red color anger,
Red color blood,
Red color murder,
Red color fury,
Red color resentfulness,
Red color warmth,
Red color lust,
Red color love,
Red color confidence,
Red color romance,
Red is energy,
Red is passion,
Red is action,
Red is desire,
Red is the root of all things humans,
Red is flip side we see in people,
Red is human,
Red will never be merely a color...

THREE

Bleeding in Kashmir

Bleeding in kashmir....
Oh! my paradise kashmir
Why are you screaming?
Why is blood shedding?
Why is every mother crying?
Why is every sister wondering?
Why is every youth fading?
Why is every foot running?
Why is every eye blaming?
Why is every heart sighing?
Why is every wise flying?
Why is every will dying?
Oh! my paradise kashmir
For what everyone is waiting?

FOUR

TEACHER FOR ME

Teacher means one who teaches us.
But for me its meaning is something else.
Mean it as the soul of mine.
Mean it as the power of my mind.
I mean it as the heart beat of mine.
I mean it as the brightness of my eyes.

For me it is the previous gift of GOD.
For me it is the future bulletin of ones life.
Thus for me it is the national pride.
For me its line is more than the love of my future time.
What importance of it i can give more than that.

Allah himself send time by time.
The prophets which gave us lesson time by time.
Thus its importance is not only in ones eyes.

But it is itself praised by GOD.
In short i want to say that;

One who teaches me a single word,
I am slave of that in all my life's time
And thus it depends upon that,
Whether that will sell me or let me free.
Still i would like to remain in the shaden of her hands....

FIVE

Be a New Person

Be a new person.
Think a new positive thought,
Dream a new dream,
But be a new person.
Write a new plan,
Build a new beautiful life,
But be a new person.
Turn a new page,
Start a new book,
But be a new person.
Light a new lantern,
Open a new door,
But be a new person.
Blaze a new trail,
Climb a new mountain,
But be a new person.
Seek a new challenge,
Find a new opportunity,
But be a new person.
Sing a new song,
Dance a new step,

But be a new person.

SIX

HOME SAFETY FOR KIDS

Many things can cause you harm,
Please be careful where you put your arm.
Kitchen ovens can cause a burn,
Many things you need to learn.

Keep in mind, sharp knives bring danger,
Never talk with any stranger.
Playing ball on the street is very bad,
If you get hurt, your mom will be sad.

Just remember, don't run down the stairs,
It's not safe, to stand on those chairs.
Be a safe kid, don't break a bone,
Don't swim without grownups or alone.

SEVEN

MY SELF

I always try to make people laugh and happy,
But no one make me.

I always tend to be friendly with people,
But everybody ignores me.

I really try to love everybody,
But no one likes me.

I pray to GOD for blessing,
But i think he is also angry with me.

My mother is my heart,
But she is not enough to support me.

My father is a great man,
But he actually doesn't understand me.

But i never lose my heart,
And i work hard.

One day time will favour me.

EIGHT

O ! GREAT GOD

O ! Great GOD
God is kind and helpful,
No doubt he is merciful,

We pray thee for thy greatness
We pray thee for the helpfulness.

All praises are for him
All letters are for him.

If we discuss his greatness
It is difficult to praise his highness.

No doubt all things are made by him
No rule is valid except of him.

Oh god why have you made the rich and the poor,
Your worship is only done by the poor,
You are always sought by the poor.

Oh! GOD of heaven and universe,

You are merciful and wise.

The rich are rich only in the world,
they are after the money always in the world.

Only the poor are my dears,
Only they are my flowers.

They pray to me that i know,
They need my help which i know......

NINE

TROUBLE

The TROUBLE keeps on coming on the MEN,
Don't be DISCOURAGED here, the world makes FUN.
The way on which you are WALKING,
there is lot of slander here,
here there is CONTROVERSY everyday.
here discussions are held in the name of RELIGIONS.
If you speak the TRUTH here, they will impose 295 section on you,
If you progress, you will get HATE here.

TEN

THE ANNUAL EXAMINATION

The Annual examination

The annual exam is on the head again
Then pass me by, I pray thee, my lord

You did me a favor last year too!
The servant was given the fruit of a year's hard work!
Then let him succeed, this is the supplication o the Lord
The annual examination is again on the head o the Lord

You remind me of every lesson I learned
But I want your kindness
Your bounties are the only hope now, O Lord
The annual exam is on the head again

Whatever you do is not your will
Man does not succeed in this
Everything is made according to your will, my lord
Yarab your servant is standing on the annual exam head

This is the prayer of "Mehvish" Yarab

ELEVEN

I ASK

I ASK

I ask you to correct the bitterness
I ask for peace and sacrifice

I beg for the joy of the torment, my friend
I ask for the same thorn in the side petal

I felt the heart of the depths
I ask for ideas from the bottom of my heart

Write on the flowing blood with the tip of a dagger
I ask for light from the liver of darkness

Let's take a look at "Mehvish"
Yes, I ask for that speed .....

TWELVE

KEEP

Keep an eye out for intense sunshine
Keep a tree for yourself

Life expectancy is very short
Keep the desires short

Every hour will be counted as one day
Be aware of every detail

The city is polluted with scandals
Hide the white face somewhere

"Mehvish" is the abode of sorrows
Keep learning each other's skills ...

THIRTEEN
THE MOTHER

The status of mother is the highest
Mother's love is the most unique

There is no one better than mother
Heaven is at his feet

The mother's heart is free from hatred
The status of mother is the highest

Its price is priceless
Which has no value

Mother is fragrant and green
The status of mother is the highest

Mother is the yard of a horse
Mother is a flower bed

Its lawn is empty of thorns
The status of mother is the highest

"Rafiqa-Farida" is my darling
The status of mother is the highest

"Mehvish" is the mother's passion
The status of mother is the highest .....

FOURTEEN
The World and My Heart

This is the world of helplessness
Tears well up in my eyes.
My heart ate my betrayal
Don't ask my heart where the pain is,

I will die of starvation now seeing the condition of my heart
Where can I take myself even if I die?
Take it from my heart, don't take revenge, where can I get my heart?

My heart is my heart My heart is my world,

I came laughing and walking in the time of sorrows
Come on in, take a look and enjoy yourself!
What is the mood of every sorrow of the heart now?
Come back, O "Mehvish" is the voice of my heart .....

FIFTEEN

EID

Eid is the day of sacrifice
Eid is a time of prosperity
Eid is the Eid of Eid prayers
Eid is Eid.

Eid is the smile on people's face
Eid is the life of every Muslim
If it were not for Eid-ul-Adha,

how could sheep and goats be sacrificed?

SIXTEEN

TODAY

Why is there a desert in my eyes today?
Why is the mirror looking at me a bit surprised,
I have been upset to see them all the time
Why is he so sorry when he is not found?
They were often found in flower gardens
Why is the same lawn so desolate today?
They used to hide their names in their hearts
Why is the same name unknown today?

SEVENTEEN

MEHVISH'S PHILOSOPHY OF LIFE

I can't find the answers to those questions
But the answer before the question is unanswerable.

I didn't get the chance to meet him
But the opportunities that come before the meeting are innumerable.

I didn't get that freedom
But those who met before independence got countless.

I did not get those dreams in my sleep
Which got my waking eyes moist.

I didn't get that laugh before I cried
But what was found after crying and laughing was not found by anyone.

I don't get that wrong knowledge "Oh God"
But the knowledge that "Mehvish" gets is better than that of the scholars.
Amen.

EIGHTEEN
COME BACK HOME

Come back home

The nest is still standing on the burning tree.
We still can reacue it,
And the chicks that wail inside.

Come back home
For it is still your own.
come back home
Let's farewell the woe.

With arm in arm,
Let's be guardians of the gates of the paradise tonight.
Tonight and forever!

Let Agha shahid sleep calmly there at northampton.
And let he not ask again
Who is the guardian tonight of the gates of paradise?

Come back home
It is still your own.
Come back home
Let's be spikes and frame it.

Half you and half we
Let's reduce to one.
Let we don't die separately,
Let you don't die at Habakadal,
And we at Fetehkadal.

Let we die together at the Gawkadal,
Where there is blood still
Glued to the shafts of early sunlight.

Half you and half we
Let's reduce to one
One hand of yours ,one ours
Let's shove and unlock sacred doors back.
Let the flare of sacred statues disperse
And captivate the peace.
Like a butterfly being captivated ,
By a just bloomed flower.

Come back home
For it is still your own.
Come back home
For it is not still too late.

The rose fragrance senses,
A thousand year's of unwashed sock now.
Even the smell of decayed dog

Sensed better than a rose fragrance
When you were here by our side.

Come back home
Let's farewell woe.
Let's be roses to eachother
And cactuses to foe.

Come back home
Cashmere is calling,
Cashmere is waiting,
Cashmere is faiding......

NINETEEN

A MIDNIGHT CALL

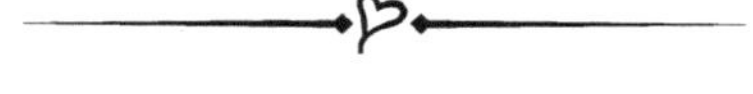

It was midnight,
Full of extreme cold and calm.
When i was on my way
To a sweet dream
Then i heard a cry
A cry which took away my sleep
A cry which hurt my heart
Yes,it was a cry of a Houseless bird.
Where is my home?
Who killed my peace?
Then i realized.....
Faulty am i and cruel.
Oh GOD! bestow me the right path
Let no one lose his home
Bird or a man,both are living.

TWENTY

MESSAGE FOR MEN

Dear men,
When a girl accepts your connection/friend request ,she accepts friendship not your proposal.
When she sends a request,she wants to be friend not the girlfriend.
When she comments ,she is sociable not flirt.
When she likes your comment,she likes the comment not you.
Respect friendship,don't search relation in it..

Biography Of Mehvish Maqbool Sanaie

Residence: Saffron Town,Pulwama,
J and k India.
Influences:Shakespeare, Rumi, Allam Iqbal, Jaun elia,etc
Marital status: Single.
Occupations:poetess, Historian, quotewriter,blogger, Gymer...

Life And Philosophy

Mehvish Maqbool Sanaie was born in the saffron town (Pampore) in the district of Pulwama in the politically disturbed state of Jammu and Kashmir in India. She is the youngest child of Mohammad Maqbool Sanaie and Fareeda Sanaie. Unlike the people around her , Mehvish has chosen the different way of leading her life. She spends most of her time reading books at her home. She has been attracted to the ideas of education, peace, love, truth, etc from the very beginning in her life. She has studied the "Holy Qur'an", the "Holy Bible". She has a good command over english, urdu, kashmiri, hindi and Turkish languages. She says that education is the best solution to all the problems of Muslims in particular and of human kind in general.

According to her, right education to Right people brings a person out of the depths of hate, anger and narrowmindedness and lifts him/her up to the zenith of love, tranquility and broadmindedness. She favours individual freedom so long as it doesn't create chaos and criticizes bitterly the outdated and rotten social constraints. Her poetry and quotes target mostly the same issues.

Once skeptical, Mehvish is now a staunch believer in Almighty Allah. She respects and honours her two local religious teachers namely Sahil sharifdin Bhat and Haseena andrabi (pakistan) who gave a unique direction to the wandering ship of her life. Mehvish, as already said, mostly loves to read books at her home. However, she occasionally loves to meet people, interacts with them on social media and sometimes, face to face and talks fun with them because she is very friendly...She is a patient listener and talks only when required . She sometimes hardly loses her cool. She is loved and respected wherever she goes, she is very kind, she is a nature lover , whoever want to talk to her he/she get mad over her, she is loyal, and she is she....Nevertheless, she too has a number of critics and unwanted foes.

Printed by Libri Plureos GmbH in Hamburg,
Germany